ELVIS

The Story of the Rock and Roll King

BONNIE CHRISTENSEN

Christy Ottaviano Books

HENRY HOLT AND COMPANY

NEW YORK

1935

EAST TUPELO, MISSISSIPPI

Things were different back then.
One door for blacks, another for whites,
whites up front, blacks in back,
right side of the tracks, wrong side of the tracks.

But music—it was everywhere.
Jazz floating between
neighborhoods,
blues chugging up both sides
of the tracks,
spirituals and gospel
pouring out of churches.

Music lifting spirits
  up
     and
        up.

Elvis Presley was born into all that music,
January 8, 1935.
One of twin baby boys, only Elvis survived.

1937

Sunday hymns raised the rafters
at First Assembly of God Church,
pulling that little Presley boy
right off his mama's lap.
Didn't know the words,
still he sure sang his heart out.

1938

Shy, quiet, dreamy boy, that Elvis.
Tied to his mama's apron strings.
No brothers, no sisters, just Elvis.
His little family kept to themselves,
poor as sin, barely getting by.

Neighbors said he cried his eyes out
when his daddy went to jail.
Elvis's mama, Gladys, lost their house,
so they kept moving, here to there.

Even after his daddy came home,
it was hard to pay the rent,
to hold on.
Gladys walked Elvis to school every day,
holding his hand,
holding on.

Elvis held on too—to music.
Black gospel, blues,
spirituals, and field songs filled the air.

Pop ballads, country and western,
even opera flowed through the radio.
Elvis loved it all.

1945

At church, Elvis sang gospel;
at school, a sad old ballad.
His teacher liked his voice so much,
she entered him in a talent show.

Shy, shaky Elvis
sang his ballad about a dog.
Didn't even have a guitar,
just sang straight through
with feeling.
Elvis won fifth place and five dollars.

1946

Gladys gave Elvis a guitar
for his eleventh birthday.
Though he never had a real lesson,
Elvis sure learned to play.
Saturdays he waited in line
for his chance on the radio.

WELO
RADIO
JAMBOREE

Kids at school wrinkled their noses,
whispered "hillbilly" and "race music."
Elvis kept right on playing,
doing what he loved best.
The family was broke though.
One night they packed up and moved on.

1948
MEMPHIS

New apartment, new school, new jobs.
Elvis's heart and soul were beating
to the rhythm of Beale Street—
and better things to come.

In his new neighborhood
Elvis found friends—
singing, guitar-picking friends.
Polite, shy Elvis
sang soft, sweet songs at twilight.
Girls liked him and his singing.

1951

High school Elvis grew sideburns,
dressed flashy, Beale Street style.
On his way to being somebody,
singing his way out.

Still, schoolkids called him "squirrely,"
put him in their talent show
for a joke.

Elvis heard their whispers and giggles.
But when he sang,
the laughing stopped,
jaws dropped.

Elvis became real popular,
for two whole months.
Then graduation.
No college for Elvis, only work,
while dreams of music filled his head.

1953
SUN RECORDS RECORDING STUDIO

Years changed while other things stayed the same—
black churches, white churches,
black radio, white radio.

Some people wanted to mix things up though,
change, cross boundaries.
Sam Phillips at Sun Records
dreamed of harmonizing black and white.
And, oh, how he loved the Delta blues.

Elvis knew all about Sun Records,
passed by the studio,
dreaming of singing, making records.

One day Elvis took the leap—
walked into the studio
and paid four dollars
to make a record.
Folks at Sun liked his voice,
unique and new,
but they didn't need a singer.

Elvis stopped by week after week.
"Need a singer?"
Week after week,
the answer was "No."
Month after month—"No."

And then . . .
Sam Phillips remembered a voice,
a singer.
What was his name?
Elvis.

July 5, 1954
SUN RECORDS

Sam and the band joked around.
Elvis twitched.

When the recording light flashed on,
Elvis sang his best,
ballads and country tunes,
this way and that.
"Not quite," Sam said.
Elvis sang his heart out, even whistled.
The sound just fell to the floor.

Sam stopped recording.
They'd take a break,
try a bit more,
then go home.

Elvis, all worry and nerves, grabbed a guitar, jumped around, singing "That's All Right."

Sam started recording.

"*That's All Right*" was a Delta blues song, and Elvis was singing it a whole new way— ragged, raw Delta blues, with bits of country and moments of gospel. Black and white music all mixed up together. A whole new sound!

WHBQ RADIO

A few days later "That's All Right" played on the radio.
Phones rang off the hook.
Everybody wanted to hear Elvis again and again.
Wanted to see him too, live on-stage.

FIRST PERFORMANCE

The band started playing,
but nervous Elvis couldn't stop shaking,
couldn't hide it either.
So he just shook with the music, moved his legs to the beat.
The audience went wild. Electricity flowed.

Elvis kept on singing,
through the Southern states,
then on to New York City
and national television.

Elvis Presley, the shy mama's boy from East Tupelo,
was on his way,
destined to become a musical legend.

With echoes of gospel, country, jazz, and blues,
Elvis's voice touched the hearts and souls of millions,
      then,
           now,
              and always.

AUTHOR'S NOTE

Vernon, Elvis, and Gladys Presley (circa 1945)

Courtesy of Getty Images

After recording "That's All Right," Elvis was on the road to stardom. Attaining stardom, however, required nearly two years of hard work constantly traveling and performing.

Elvis and his band (Winfield "Scotty" Moore on guitar and Bill Black on double bass) sometimes played as many as four shows a day before traveling to the next town for the next show. They often performed every day of the week, taking only a day or two off when they didn't have a booking.

The endless touring paid off. In 1955 Elvis signed a contract with RCA Records, one of the biggest record companies in the United States. He acquired a manager, Colonel Tom Parker, who booked him on radio and television shows and helped launch his career. Elvis soon became a household name, often referred to as the King of Rock and Roll or simply The King.

During the course of his career, Elvis recorded one hundred forty-one albums and singles, and sold over one billion records worldwide, more than any other performer. One hundred thirty-one Elvis recordings earned gold, platinum, or multiplatinum awards from the record industry. Elvis starred and sang in thirty-one major movies during his career. He was nominated fourteen times for the Grammy Award and won three times.

Elvis's generosity is a legend. He gave lavish gifts to family and friends and performed numerous concerts to benefit charities. Through the Elvis Presley Charitable Foundation and the work of his worldwide fan clubs, Elvis's generosity endures.

President Jimmy Carter said, "His music and his personality, fusing the styles of white country and black rhythm and blues, permanently changed the face of American popular culture. His following was immense, and he was a symbol to people the world over of the vitality, rebelliousness, and good humor of his country."

"Elvis is the greatest cultural force in the twentieth century. He introduced the beat to everything— music, language, clothes; it's a whole new social revolution—the '60s comes from it."
—LEONARD BERNSTEIN

TIME LINE

January 8, 1935
Jesse Garon and Elvis Aron (later Aaron), twins, born to Gladys and Vernon Presley in East Tupelo, Mississippi. Only Elvis survives.

May 25, 1938
Vernon Presley is sentenced to three years in prison for forging a check. He serves only eight months.

October 3, 1945
Elvis performs in a talent contest at the state fair sponsored by Tupelo radio station WELO. He wears glasses and wins fifth place.

January 8, 1946
Elvis gets his first guitar as a birthday present.

November 6, 1948
The Presleys move to Memphis in search of work and a better life.

June 3, 1953
Elvis graduates from Humes High School.

July 5, 1954
Elvis, with Scotty Moore and Bill Black, records "That's All Right" at Sun Records.

November 21, 1955
RCA signs Elvis to a record contract.

March 23, 1956
Elvis's first album, *Elvis Presley*, is released by RCA.

March 26, 1956
Colonel Tom Parker becomes Elvis's manager.

April 3, 1956
Elvis performs for the first time on national television on *The Milton Berle Show*. Later in 1956 he performs again on *The Milton Berle Show* and then on *The Steve Allen Show* and *The Ed Sullivan Show*.

November 21, 1956
Love Me Tender, Elvis's first movie, is released.

March 25, 1957
Elvis buys Graceland, an estate that remains his family's Memphis home for twenty years.

March 24, 1958
Elvis is inducted into the U.S. Army. He is stationed in Friedberg, Germany, where he meets Priscilla Beaulieu.

August 14, 1958
Gladys Presley, Elvis's mother dies; he is inconsolable.

March 5, 1960
Elvis is honorably discharged from the army.

1960–1967
Elvis stars in 27 movies during this period, averaging about three movies a year.

May 1, 1967
Elvis and Priscilla Beaulieu are married.

February 1, 1968
Lisa Marie is born to Elvis and Priscilla.

December 3, 1968
NBC airs Elvis's first live performance since 1961, the *'68 Comeback Special*. The show has the highest ratings of the television season.

1970–1973
Elvis begins touring and recording again; he signs a five-year contract to perform regularly at the largest venue in Las Vegas.

October 9, 1973
Elvis and Priscilla divorce.

1973–1977
Despite medical and emotional problems, Elvis continues performing and recording. He records six albums.

August 16, 1977
Elvis dies at Graceland at the age of 42.

SOURCES

Guralnick, Peter. *Last Train to Memphis: The Rise of Elvis Presley*. Boston: Little, Brown, 1994.

Guralnick, Peter, and Ernst Jorgensen. *Elvis Day by Day*. New York: Ballantine, 1999.

Mason, Bobbie Ann. *Elvis Presley*. New York: Viking, 2003.

For my friends in Wilson, North Carolina, with love and appreciation
for your acceptance, kindness, and amazing grace

Henry Holt and Company, LLC, *Publishers since 1866*
175 Fifth Avenue, New York, New York 10010 • mackids.com

Henry Holt® is a registered trademark of Henry Holt and Company, LLC.

Library of Congress Cataloging-in-Publication Data
Christensen, Bonnie.
Elvis : the story of the rock and roll King / Bonnie Christensen.—First edition.
pages   cm
Includes bibliographical references.
ISBN 978-0-8050-9447-3 (hardcover)
1. Presley, Elvis, 1935–1977—Juvenile literature. 2. Rock musicians—United States—Biography—Juvenile literature. I. Title.
ML3930.P73C47 2015   782.42166092—dc23   [B]   2014024990

Henry Holt books may be purchased for business or promotional use. For information on bulk purchases, please contact the
Macmillan Corporate and Premium Sales Department at (800) 221-7945 x5442 or by e-mail at specialmarkets@macmillan.com.

First Edition—2015 / Designed by Patrick Collins
The art for this book was created using traditional photo collage, which was then scanned, printed on paper, and painted with oils.
Printed in China by South China Printing Co. Ltd., Dongguan City, Guangdong Province

1 3 5 7 9 10 8 6 4 2